SHARKS AND TROUBLED WATERS

by
Margaret Harris

A

Book

From

RAINTREE CHILDRENS BOOKS
Milwaukee • Toronto • Melbourne • London

Library of Congress Number: 77-10760

Art and Photo Credits

Cover illustration by Lynn Sweat.
Illustrations on pages 7, 17, 18, 40, and 48, Meredith Kurtzman.
Photos on pages 10 and 33, Scott Ransom/Taurus Photos.
Photo on page 12, Sea Library, Ben Cropp.
Photos on pages 13 and 34, Ron and Valerie Taylor/Bruce Coleman, Inc.
Photos on pages 15, 29, and 45, Wide World Photos.
Photo on page 22, Peter A. Lake, Sea Library.
Photo on page 26, Consulate General of Japan, N.Y.
Photo on page 37, Tom McHugh/Photo Researchers, Inc.
Photo on page 39, Howard Sochurek, Woodfin Camp & Associates.
Photo on page 41, Doug Wallin/Taurus Photos.
Photo on page 47, Norman Owen Tomalin/Bruce Coleman, Inc.
All photo research for this book was provided by Sherry Olan.
Every effort has been made to trace the ownership of all copyrighted material in this
book and to obtain permission for its use.

Library of Congress Cataloging in Publication Data

Harris, Margaret, 1935-
    Sharks and troubled waters.
    SUMMARY: Discusses facts and myths that have contributed to the
fear and respect humans have for sharks.
    1. Sharks—Juvenile literature. [1. Sharks] I. Title.
QL638.9.H37 597'.31 77-10760
ISBN 0-8172-1041-5 lib. bdg.

Manufactured in the United States of America
ISBN 0-8172-1041-5

CONTENTS

Chapter

1

SHARKS AND SHIPWRECKS

The sea was calm. *Too calm. Too quiet.* The boat seemed not to move at all. The wind had died. All that was left in its place was a soft breeze. There were only the sounds of creaking timbers and the flapping of useless sails.

Not a word was said among the crew. All eyes now watched the bright blue sky become darker and darker, until it was the color of lead. Whitecaps appeared, breaking the smooth surface of the ocean. The choppy waters grew into rolling waves that threw the small sailing ship from side to side.

The silence was suddenly broken by the captain. Looking up toward the approaching storm, he barked, "Take in all sail but the main stay-sail." The pounding of running feet on the wooden deck was soon drowned out by wind and rain. The storm was upon them.

Winds and rain beat furiously upon the ship. Within minutes, the crew was holding onto the ropes to keep from falling overboard. Then came a cry from the lookout. *"Reef ahead!"* But it was too late. The ship crashed on the rocks with the force of an explosion. The men on the ropes were thrown into the sea. Wave after wave tossed the ship against the reef. Those still on deck were washed overboard. All at once, the whole ship seemed to tear apart.

A dark fin streaked through the water. Then another—and another! Soon there were so many that the men in the water wished they had been the first to die. The shark pack circled, swimming slowly, almost lazily. Around and around they swam in smaller and smaller circles. The sharks were closing in on the helpless men.

One by one, the sharks broke away from the pack. They would head directly for one of the men and then suddenly move away at the last second. Again and again one of the huge blue sharks would dart among the men as if choosing its target. The terrified men, holding fast to floating chunks of their broken ship, could only wait. *They didn't have to wait long!*

Thrown overboard, the men swam helplessly in the stormy sea.

In a tremendous rush, one of the sharks attacked. A terrible scream was heard. The shark seemed to leap half out of the water, a torn body in its jaws. The scent of blood in the water set off a feeding frenzy that left not a single survivor from the ill-fated ship.

Stories of shipwrecks have been repeated countless times in the thousands of years that people have sailed the seas. A part of almost every story told is the shadowy shape of the killer shark. The shark has been hated by some and worshipped by others. But one thing is certain—*the shark has always been feared.*

Chapter

2

SHARKS: THE PERFECT HUNTERS

There is no creature in the sea more terrifying than the shark. People have had superstitions and made up myths about sharks that have been passed along for centuries. Stories have been told of sharks large enough to smash holes in the sides of great ships. Sharks have been said to hurl themselves from the water to snatch some poor sailor from his boat.

Magical stories of old Hawaii tell of killer sharks who can change into human form, destroy their enemies, and then return to the sea as sharks. Even today, these ancient creatures of the sea are thought by some to be cruel, ever-hungry hunters of human flesh. These are some of the myths. What is the truth about sharks?

Sharks were among the earliest animals on earth. We know there were sharks swimming

The great white shark is one of the most dangerous of the killer sharks.

the oceans at least 140 million years ago. While no shark bodies this old have been found, fossil teeth of prehistoric sharks have been discovered. Teeth from the *great white shark* have been found that are six inches long. There are people who believe these triangle-shaped teeth are from sharks 80 to 90 feet long. Sharks this size would have huge jaws capable of swallowing a Volkswagon!

As exciting as the idea of a 90-foot shark sounds, it probably isn't true. The largest fish in the world is a shark—the whale shark—that sometimes grows to almost 65 feet in length. The whale shark is not a flesh-eater. It feeds on ocean plants and small fish.

Norwegian adventurer Thor Heyerdahl once met up with the *whale shark.* On his sailing voyage from Peru to Polynesia, Heyerdahl and his crew spotted fish "bigger than elephants." In fact, at one point during his trip, Heyerdahl said one of these giant monsters was visible from both sides of the boat at the same time. The largest known flesh-eating shark measures about 40 feet. Standing on its tail a shark this size would stretch up as tall as a four-story building.

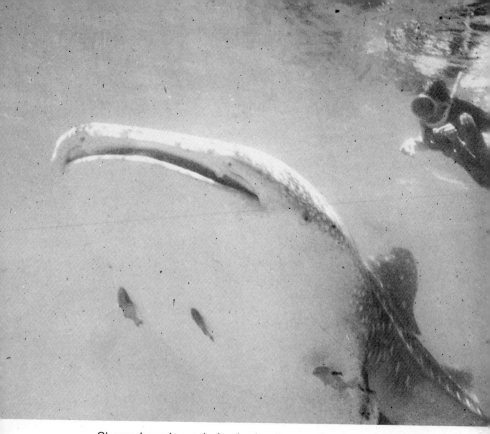

Shown here is a whale shark—the gentle giant of the seas.

Perhaps the 90-foot monster of man's imagination *did* exist at one time. But there is no proof. That monster shark remains a legend. On the other hand, there *are* fossil teeth that probably came from a race of killer sharks that must have been more than 60 feet long. Killers that size no longer roam the seas.

Sharks are not bony fish. Their bodies are made up of *cartilage*—the kind of firm, rubbery material that forms the tip of your nose. The dead shark's body, therefore, decays quickly and leaves no fossil bones for scientists to study. What we know of the age and life of sharks comes from studies of fossil teeth and living creatures.

The shark has been called "the perfect hunter." A major reason is the shark's jaw and its several rows of teeth. Most rows are slanted toward the rear of the mouth. Each row is slightly larger than the last. When the shark bites, its

Flashing rows of sharp teeth, this great white shark opens his huge jaws as he attacks the camera.

sharp, sawlike teeth easily slice through tough flesh. The angled rear teeth hold on fast to the victim. It is easy to get something into a shark's mouth but impossible to get it back out. The shark always has its original number of teeth. As a tooth is lost, another grows to replace it. A *tiger shark* is said to grow 24,000 individual teeth over a ten-year period of time.

In addition to the jaw, the shark's entire body makes it "the perfect hunter." Its sleek, smooth form is as streamlined as a torpedo for speedy movement through the water. Sharks swim more than 30 knots an hour (equal to land speeds of almost 35 mph). In the words of Jacques Cousteau, famous underwater explorer: "[the shark body] is fluid, weaving from side to side . . . his head moves slowly from left to right, right to left, timed to the rhythm of his motion through the water. Only the [shark's] eye is fixed . . . on me in order not to lose sight, for a fraction of a second, of his enemy."

Not all sharks are killers. There are some, like the giant whale sharks, that actually refuse to attack people. Stories are told of sailors taunting these sharks—daring them to attack. Even this did not make the whale sharks angry. In

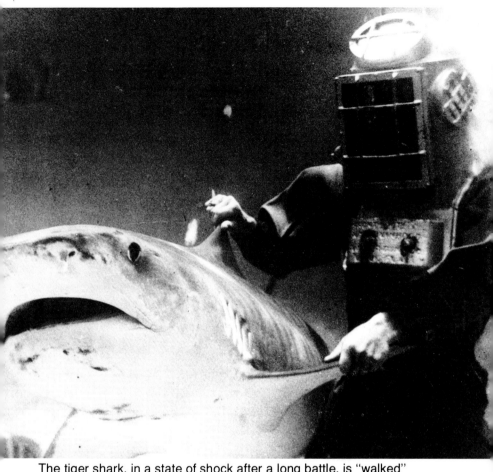

The tiger shark, in a state of shock after a long battle, is "walked" by his captor. This keeps the shark from drowning by forcing fresh water through its mouth and gills. When the shark recovers, the diver will move away—*fast*!

fact, whale sharks will go out of their way to avoid bumping into small boats or divers.

The Bible tells the story of Jonah who was swallowed by a big fish. Jonah tried to flee from the Lord and took passage on a ship going to a

15

port called Tarshish. But the Lord caused a great wind and mighty waves. The ship was in danger of sinking.

Jonah told the men to cast him into the sea and it would be calm. Still, the men tried to row toward shore. But the storm became worse, and they could not make their way to safety. So the men threw Jonah into the sea. And the sea became calm. Then the Lord sent a great fish to swallow up Jonah. Jonah prayed inside the fish, and the Lord caused the fish to cough up Jonah upon the dry land.

We have usually heard this story called "Jonah and the Whale." But this Biblical story speaks of a very big *fish*. This fish was able to hold Jonah in its body and spit up just the man, holding onto the other food it had eaten. The whale is not a fish but a *mammal*. Perhaps Jonah was really swallowed by a large whale shark rather than a whale. Sharks can store food for a time without digesting it. They can also throw up one thing they have eaten without giving up other food they have eaten.

Sharks have been known to swallow a lot of less likely things than Jonah. Sharks have been

Could the sea monster that swallowed Jonah have been a whale shark, rather than a whale?

called "swimming garbage cans"—and with good reason. Among the more unusual things found in their stomachs have been cans of nails, telephone books, pots, a carpenter's square, and a 30-foot long roll of roofing paper!

A shark caught off the coast of Australia had some even more amazing things in its stomach.

There was half a ham, two legs of mutton, the hind quarters of a pig, and the head of a bulldog with a rope still tied around its neck. The stomach of another shark, captured in the Adriatic Sea, held three overcoats, a nylon raincoat, and an automobile license plate!

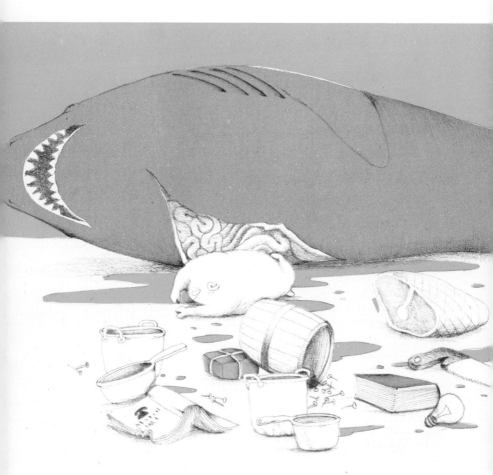

Many strange things have been found in the stomachs of sharks.

While sharks often swallow some very strange things, they can also be quite fussy about what they eat. Sharks will accept a free meal of fresh garbage, especially if hunting has been poor, but scientists have learned that sharks will not accept spoiled meat unless they are starving. They much prefer fresh fish and fresh meat. The killer shark is said even to go after other sharks in a *feeding frenzy.*

It is this last thought—the feeding frenzy of the sharks—that strikes terror in the hearts of those who sail or swim in the sea. And it is this terror that has made many humans into shark hunters.

Chapter

3

SAVAGE FURY

The water churned with the thrashing of sharks. The men in the boats threw over bucket after bucket of *chum*—ground-up fish used by fishermen as bait. The smell of the fish brought sharks from miles around the boat. Now, the sharks were in a frenzy—a feeding frenzy—that would not stop until they swallowed every fish chunk they could find. Fighting each other for the free meal, smaller sharks were slashed and eaten by bigger ones. The ocean was like a bubbling cauldron, red with blood. The sharks tore each other to pieces in their madness. The men gloried in the death struggle that they were witnessing.

Heavy fishing lines were dropped over the side of the boat. Some sharks were hauled aboard. The men cut out the snapping jaws of the sharks as souvenirs of the slaughter. Rifles were brought up from below the deck. Shots echoed across the water, bullets moving clean through the dark skin of the feeding giants. Again and again, guns exploded. The men were trying to destroy as many sharks as possible.

What deep, terrible fear drove the men to kill sharks, not for food, but for fun? Was it some ancient fear of the sharks' mysterious powers? Was it simply to rid the area of some terrible danger from too many sharks? Just how dangerous is the shark?

Sharks are dangerous to people, not just because they are vicious hunters, but because of people's beliefs about sharks. Many who think they know about sharks often ignore their very *real* dangers. For example, it is widely believed that sharks can only bite when they turn themselves belly up. Who knows how many swimmers and divers have died because of this belief?

Although sharks can bite in an upside-down position, they usually don't. They like a straight-on attack. The shark's mouth is placed way back under its long snout. But when the shark opens its mouth, the lower jaw moves forward while the upper jaw moves up and back. In this new position the mouth is no longer under the shark's body, it is right in front of the head.

Shark jaws are often prized as fearsome souvenirs.

Many people still believe "old wives' tales" about the shark's poor eyesight. The poor divers who believe that sharks don't see well have not lived to tell about it. Sharks, as other sea animals, see well at a distance. They also use their powerful senses of smell and hearing about the same way we do on land. The difference is that these senses are not the shark's only important hunting equipment.

"The perfect hunter" finds out what and *who* is around to be eaten through a very sensitive "feeling" system. The shark "feels" movements in the water around it. The shark body contains a *lateral line*—a series of liquid-filled channels under the skin that are connected to the outside by tiny tubes. The canals are dotted with nerve cells that send messages to the brain. These messages tell the shark about movement in the water for distances up to 100 feet or so.

In the silent world of the sea, animals are hunted every minute of the day. Most sea animals avoid problems by moving without making any sound at all. But any movement—no matter how silent—changes the pressure of the water around the swimmer. It is this change in pressure that the deadly shark feels. Combined with a huge appetite, this feeling of pressure change will likely be followed by a quick and sudden attack.

Experiments have been done to test the shark's ability to sense movements in the water. Sharks have been attracted from behind solid rock walls by a hard clapping of the hands. It is thought that people swimming and splashing at beaches send out these same pressure signals. These signals cause the shark to attack, but they are not the only signals for a hungry shark. The shark has an incredible sense of smell. The nostrils of the shark are like grooves in its head. They are set wide apart, and as the shark swims, the water runs across the nostrils in a steady stream. With the water comes the scent of the shark's prey.

Because the two nostrils are so far apart, the shark can easily tell which one is picking up the strongest odor. The shark then swims in that direction. The shark's sense of smell helps it to follow some poor creature for miles across the sea, especially when the creature is wounded and leaking blood into the water. Once onto the scent, a shark's sense of direction is deadly accurate. Many a sick or wounded fish, many a shipwrecked or torpedoed sailor has witnessed the shark's keen sense of direction!

Spear fishermen are often killed by sharks who probably did not really want to attack a dangerous-looking human in the first place. But poorly informed spear fishermen attach the fish they spear to belts tied around their waist. This leaves a perfect trail of fish scent and blood for "the perfect hunter" to follow. Wise spear fishermen will hand the speared fish and the gun up to someone in a boat to avoid attracting sharks.

A variety of anti-shark devices have been invented to protect divers and swimmers from shark attacks. Special rods, or "billies," with points at the end to keep sharks at a distance, special cages, and screens are all being tested. But, for years, people who must dive into shark-filled waters to earn their living have used their own means of keeping sharks from attacking. Some spear fishermen leave their catch on long ropes, floating behind them. Often, sharks will attack only the fish, leaving the fishermen alone. If that sounds pretty risky to you, you're right!

The Japanese *ama* divers, men and women who dive for abalone, have an unusual way of warding off shark attacks. These divers wrap a six- to eight-foot red cloth around them. A red tail of cloth trails them when they dive into the water. It was once thought that the red color warded off shark attacks. No one knows whether it is the color or the length of the cloth that works. But sharks do not usually bother the *ama* divers.

The Japanese Ama divers aren't usually bothered by sharks.

Chapter

4

THE FEEDING FRENZY

The purple light of dawn shone on the smooth ocean water in small, bouncing specks of light. One of a crew of scientists fished from the back of the large boat. He was bringing in the catch of the day—part of it for fresh food, part for tempting sharks. The scientists were sailing in the area of a large coral reef known to be the hiding place—and the hunting grounds—of enormous packs of killer sharks.

Fishing had been good in the early hours of the morning—lots of tuna and barracuda were already on board. Yawning, the scientist was about to reel in his empty fishing line when he felt an enormous tug at the end of the line. He pulled hard and the rod in his hands bent almost in two. No doubt of it, he had just landed something that was mighty big. For the next five minutes, it was a battle between man and fish. The fish fought hard, lunging from side to side trying to unhook itself from the line.

Suddenly, a familiar shape broke through the water behind the struggling fish that was fighting for its life. The familiar shape was the fin of a shark following the prey some helpful human had trapped with a fishing hook. At first, the shark merely followed its struggling target. Then, as the captive fish began to weaken, the scientist started to "bring him in."

The shark moved so quickly, it could have been shot from a cannon. It moved straight in on the huge fish, seeming not even to have slowed as it swam right by. When the fish was finally hauled into the boat, it was little more than a bloody head. Its body had been sawed in two by a shark in less time than it takes to tell about it!

The crew of scientists on the boat, led by Jacques Cousteau, lowered a steel cage into the water. Through the steel bars several items could be seen inside the cage. There was a television camera, several pounds of freshly caught fish (the shark bait caught earlier), a spear gun,

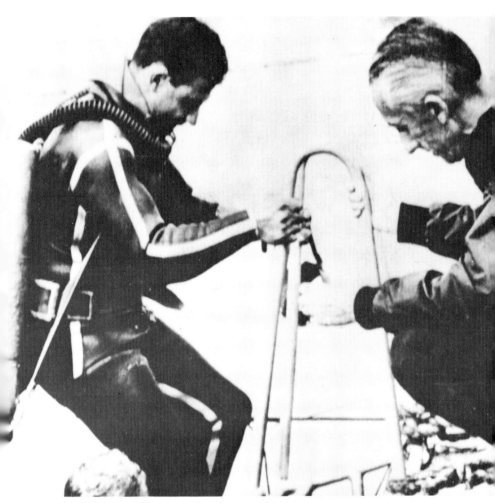

From the deck of his boat "Calypso," Jacques Cousteau (right) watches his diver go below.

and *one human being* wearing the gear of a deep-water diver!

As the cage was lowered, about a dozen dark, sleek shapes swam slowly around it in a wide circle. The cage settled on the ocean floor. A huge turtle swam in close to the cage, ignoring the circling pack which had now increased in number to about 50. The diver opened the door, stepped from the cage, and turned it so that the rays of sunlight would strike him and the fish. *He was making himself an easy target for the sharks to see!*

Back inside the cage, the man now began to push chunks of fish through the bars. An enormous *grouper* fish swam up and snatched up the fish instantly. Still the sharks circled at a distance from the cage. The *grouper* grabbed up a final morsel offered from the cage—a large *barracuda*. The satisfied *grouper* seemed to decide this would be a good time to leave. It turned and slowly moved away from the still unfed sharks.

Now there were several sharks swimming close to the cage. They were still moving in a circle, and each second brought more sharks into the pack. Hundreds of them now moved around the cage. When the sharks got close enough, the diver speared their fins with brightly colored tags. These markers would help keep track of this pack of sharks if and when they moved to new ocean homes in the future.

The man in the cage threw fish snacks out, and some of the sharks broke from their circle to snatch them up. Excitement was beginning to build among the circling hunters. More and more sharks began to swim from the pack. Suddenly, one shark—about six feet long—struck out at another, trying to pull away the small colored tag that had been speared through its fin. More and more fish chunks were being hurled from the cage, and the sharks soon reached the point of frenzy. They tore at the fish and at each other, fighting for the small prizes of food.

There were more sharks than the man had ever thought there would be. They were out of control—*powerful hunters gone mad!* Biting at anything in sight, several sharks hurled themselves at the steel cage, trying to get at the fish inside.

Whipping their fins, turning their bodies sharply, the sharks were battering the steel bars that stood between them and the meal they were after. The lone *live* meal inside the cage was now worried that the bars might crack under the crushing weight of frenzied sharks. But suddenly the diver had a much greater problem. He was no longer the only living thing inside the cage.

How it had happened, no one knew, but a shark had forced its way into the cage. The man turned his only weapon—the spear—on the killer. On the boat above, the rest of the crew watched the fight on the television screens, not knowing how to help the diver so many feet below on the ocean floor.

The caged man pushed the point of his spear again and again at the shark. He succeeded in beating the shark off when suddenly another shark plunged his head between the bars and snatched the sack of fish from the cage. What luck! Not only did the rest of the pack follow the sack of fish away from the cage, but the shark inside squeezed back through the bent bars to chase the fish that had stolen the prize.

As the fish started to swim away, the dazed diver threw his twisted spear into the body of a small shark. Those watching the television screens waited breathlessly for the next feeding

As the camera focused on him, the shark approached the cage.

frenzy when the sharks would turn to attack one of their own—now wounded. Long-held beliefs about sharks said this would happen. Sharks are supposed to attack one of their own when it is wounded and trailing blood. But this did not happen. The sharks slowed their speed and now swam in a circle a good distance from the cage.

The killer shark seemed determined to attack.

The man in the cage speared a passing *red snapper*. The fish was large and freed itself from the spear. Wounded, it started to limp off. In an instant, its back was torn open by the flashing teeth of a shark. Once more the water was alive with charging, twisting sharks tearing apart a wounded, bloody red snapper. The feeding frenzy was on again. The sharks would battle each other in a rage until the last bit of red snapper was gone.

What causes the feeding frenzy of the sharks? Why would they not attack their own when it was wounded? Why are so many human beliefs about the shark—one of the earth's oldest creatures—so often wrong? Are sharks really unpredictable?

Chapter
5

SHARK MYTHS AND SUPERSTITIONS

To most people in the world, the shark has always been a monster of mystery. Perhaps this is because so many species of sharks have been able to survive since prehistoric ages. The giant prehistoric reptiles—the dinosaurs, the plesiosaurs—were all replaced by smaller land mammals, but the shark has somehow lived on.

Some think the shark is brilliant and indestructible—the ruler of the seas. The shark seems to swim its way around the world, at will, often leaving the salt water of oceans for the

fresh water of lakes and rivers. As with all superstitions, these beliefs are sometimes based on
little fact and much ignorance.

In Nicaragua, Central America, the *bull
shark* seems quite at home in the fresh water of

The bull shark makes its home in the fresh waters
of Lake Nicaragua.

Lake Nicaragua. The bull shark is also the supreme being in the lake. It attacks with quick and fatal results.

The people of Lake Nicaragua have great fear and respect for the sharks that swim in their lake. When some Nicaraguans die, their relatives dress their bodies with jewelry and throw them to the sharks. This Nicaraguan superstition has given the bull shark an unfortunate appetite for human flesh. It has also made swimming in the lake a dangerous sport.

A "foreigner" to the area thought he could make his fortune on the superstition behind this strange Nicaraguan burial. He decided to steal the jewelry that lies at the bottom of the watery graveyard. The grave robber made some dives and was well on his way to becoming a rich man. Then one day he did not return from a "treasure dive." His sudden disappearance left no doubt that he provided a live dinner for the sharks. The superstition of the Nicaraguans had come back to haunt the fortune hunter.

While sharks have adapted to fresh water and other unbelievable changes, they do not seem to move from place to place. Cousteau and

To avoid the bull sharks, some people have built pools for swimming on the tiny islands of the lake.

others have tagged sharks to see how often they moved to other areas of the world. The ocean scientists have found that most sharks, especially the reef sharks, stay pretty much in one area all

Could wearing a tattoo of a shark's jaw ward off sharks?

their lives. They move when they are forced to by sudden danger—usually from human shark hunters.

Sharks have always been surrounded by superstitions. The people of the Red Sea strike two stones together to ward off attacks. In the Pacific Islands, this method is used to *attract* sharks.

In 16th century Europe, the sight of a *hammerhead shark* was a sign of bad luck. Yet,

A hammerhead shark makes a strange underwater sight.

at this same period in history, shark "good-luck charms" were widely used in other areas of the world. The tail of a shark was nailed to sailing ships to ward off danger. In Australia, shark giants were blamed for shipwrecks. Shark teeth, which were once feared for their destructive powers are, today, set in gold necklaces to bring the wearer good luck.

Chapter

6

WHO CAN SCARE A SHARK?

Is the shark the "king of the sea"? Is "the perfect hunter" ever, itself, the *hunted?* The answers are *no* and *yes.* While it's true that sharks have survived long after other prehistoric monsters on the land were overtaken by smaller mammals, the sharks have had their problems too. They are often powerless to overcome some of the warm-blooded mammals of the sea.

The dolphin is not a fish, although it spends its life in the water. The dolphin is a mammal,

43

just as you and I. It is warm-blooded while fish are cold-blooded. It has completely adapted to life in the sea, probably having once been a land animal. In fact, because the dolphin once lived on the land, it has a strong vertebral column. It swims at great speeds and can move almost straight up or down in the water. The dolphin breathes air and must, at times, rise quickly to the surface of the ocean.

Most people think of the dolphin as a cute, playful, bright sea animal. But the dolphin is in many ways stronger than the shark. It can swim longer and farther than the shark because its warm blood circulates to its muscles more completely than the cold blood of the shark. The dolphin has a "sounding" system that warns of approaching dangers. It is usually ready for the shark when an attack comes.

Finally, the dolphin is *smart*—a great deal smarter than the shark. The dolphins live in groups that sound messages and warnings to one another. The dolphins plan actions for the whole group to outwit their enemies.

Sharks don't usually attack healthy dolphins. Although the shark's jaw is better for tearing and slicing during an attack, the dolphin's jaw has smaller teeth for catching and holding fish. But the dolphin's long, pointed snout is so strong

The gentle-looking dolphin can often out-wit the shark. Here, a dolphin family goes for a swim.

that the dolphin can beat a shark to death by striking hard blows at the shark's body.

Another mammal of the sea that sharks usually don't bother is the dreaded *killer whale*. Small, compared with other whales, the killer whale is a warm-blooded, powerful mammal and, like the dolphin, it swims quickly up and down in the ocean (the whale must also breathe air to live). Killer whales are known to dart from deep waters straight up under the shark's belly, clenching the surprised shark in a "death grip" between powerful whale jaws—jaws more powerful even than those of the killer shark.

No, the shark is not indestructible. It is, however, a dangerous foe to that land-living mammal who ventures into the ocean—the human.

Superstitions about the shark are made from the same recipes as most superstitions. They begin with people's fears. Add to those fears, heavy doses of ignorance and a pinch of imagination, and you have it. But maybe superstitions about the shark are less awful and more forgivable than most other superstitions. The people who have studied these dangerous creatures all their lives

A killer whale shows off his powerful jaws and sharp teeth.

tell us the shark *is* absolutely unpredictable. And there is no question that in "the perfect hunter" we have found something truly worth fearing.

There was the ancient belief that the mighty shark was given magical powers by Poseidon, the ancient Greek god of the sea.

DATE DUE

JAN 1 0 '80			
MAY 1 5 '89			
APR 0 2 '92			
JUN 0 1 '92			
MAR 2 3 '93			
APR 2 8 '94			
APR 2 8 '95			
DEC 1 8 '95			
MAR 11 '96			
APR 24 96			
MAY 13 '98			
MAY 29 '98			
GAYLORD			PRINTED IN U.S.A